Copyright © 2020 by Lawrence Hughes

ISBN: 978-1-7365017-0-2

Table of Contents

INTRODUCTION

King David is a familiar and fascinating character to many of us. He famously defeated the feared Philistine warrior Goliath, armed with only a sling and five stones. He was a musician, who played the lyre to soothe the first king of Israel, Saul. He was a poet, credited for writing at least 73 of the 150 expressions of praise to God in the Old Testament's book of Psalms. David, who served as king of Judah and then all of Israel for forty years, led the armies of Israel to many victories over the armies of many city-states during his reign. David also provided much of the material and resources required for his son, King Solomon, to construct the great First Temple in Jerusalem. Scripture informs us that David, whose lineage of descendants includes Jesus Christ, had an unshakable love for and faith in God. 1 Samuel 13:14 (King James Version) declares that God saw David as "a man after his own (God's) heart ..."

But we also know David as a flawed man; one who fell prey to the same fears, emotions, and temptations to which all men and women fall prey. We know that David abused his power and authority to commit adultery with Bathsheba. We also know he committed murder in order to cover up his adulterous behavior. David was far from the perfect man or perfect leader.

But it is *not* my intention to draw leadership insights from only the noble and virtuous behaviors he exhibited in life. On the contrary, the insights I will offer have been extracted from both positive behaviors and behaviors that illustrate what we should seek to avoid. The six lessons offered in this book are not intended to be a tribute to David or a call to faith. This is a work that draws experiences from the life of David that can inform how we lead teams or contribute to those teams. It is important that I declare this writing is not just for those leaders who have direct reports assigned to them. I believe everyone can choose to be a leader in their organization, whether they are assigned to a managerial role or as an individual contributor. Let me clearly state that the lessons offered in this book should be viewed as beneficial to both.

I am not a theologian. I am not a graduate of a seminary. Nor did I take any courses on the Bible or religion in college. But I have already noted that this book is not written to inform your spiritual life. It is designed to offer leaders in team settings some constructs that may enhance their effectiveness. It offers a set of leadership lessons that, when embraced and lived out, will add value to your team's output. Yet even with that disclaimer, you may be wondering who I am and why you should listen to anything I have to offer.

I am a leader with nearly forty years of organizational leadership and managerial experience. My leadership experiences began when I entered West Point as a cadet in the summer of 1982. I recall my four years at the United States Military Academy as four years in a leadership laboratory. From day one, I began to learn lessons related to the importance of listening intently, being precise in my communications, ensuring both the sender and receiver of messages are on the same page, taking accountability for my actions and inactions, and taking accountability for the actions of those I am charged with leading. There are too many lessons from West Point to enumerate in an introductory chapter. But most importantly, West Point ignited a passion in me to seek out leadership lessons in every situation and to apply those lessons for the betterment of the team.

My education in and practice of leadership continued beyond my graduation from West Point and into the army, where I was first assigned as a platoon leader in a field artillery unit. My military leadership experiences over the next eight years included leadership in both active duty and national guard components of the United States Army. These leadership experiences culminated in back-to-back company-level command assignments.

Outside the military, I have led in both large public company and smaller not-for-profit environments. My leadership assignments have included accountability for teams delivering annual revenues ranging from $35 million to more than $2 billion. I have led at the district level, regional level, divisional level, and zone level in corporate environments. I have also led a small not-for-profit practice where I aligned both university and community resources to assist small businesses to accelerate their growth. I have led corporate learning and development functions, the franchise systems function for one of the largest franchising organizations in the world, veteran's outreach programs, and diversity and inclusion efforts at a multi-billion dollar company. I have taught leadership, strategy, and organizational behavior in university environments, and I have served as a director on numerous not-for-profit governing boards. My experiences include serving as the founding board chair of Degrees of Change, an organization that prepares underrepresented college students from urban neighborhoods to become leaders in their communities. But most importantly, alongside Angela, my wife of over thirty years, I have shepherded

Geoffrey and Garrett, my twenty-something-year-old sons, through their life journeys.

So, what does this mean? Why am I sharing this background with you at the beginning of this work? I am doing this to affirm for you that I have observed and experienced a number of behaviors and dynamics that tend to lead to organizational success from both managerial and individual contributor roles. I have also seen behaviors that, more often than not, tend to detract from, or even completely derail, success from those same roles. The latter set of behaviors tend to create unnecessary turbulence among the team. If I am to be completely transparent, I have engaged in both the productive and nonproductive behaviors, and I have experienced both the positive and not-so-positive outcomes.

I am sharing this with you because we learn from both successes and from setbacks. I would even argue that we tend to learn more from setbacks than from successes. While I will leave it to the industrial psychologists to provide the detailed support for that dynamic, I will simply hypothesize that we do a lot more reflection around individual behaviors, interpersonal dynamics, system capabilities, and external forces when our efforts produce outcomes that didn't meet our expectations. And quite frankly, I would be suspect of any person sharing leadership gems if that person had never experienced organizational difficulties. I have grown from my setbacks and they have equipped me with deeper leadership insight.

I have always believed that I have an obligation as a leader to help others be more effective leaders on teams that they lead or serve. It only made sense to me that I should take the next step and share some leadership insights with those beyond the boundaries of my organization and professional network. And because these lessons are not tied to one's faith or spiritual beliefs, they can be applied by leaders of all faith backgrounds, and by those who embrace no faith at all.

Perhaps another question you have is, "Why only six leadership lessons?" "Is there some magic around the number six?" While there is no magic around the number six, I hope this book becomes a practical, usable tool for you in your workplace. I have discovered that oftentimes, less can be more when offering tips and challenges. When I travel to my retail stores, I find that bombarding them with too many ideas can be more confusing and less practical than offering a few big ideas they can get their arms around. The beauty of six lessons lies in their actionability. They are not too many nor too few.

The six lessons I present to you are valuable for new leaders, as well as experienced leaders, who are looking to expand their leadership tool kits. Even if you do not supervise others, the lessons can help you be more effective as a contributor to your team. I have arranged the lessons into a framework, I call the LEADER framework, which will help you remember the lessons you explore in each chapter. The LEADER framework is:

L – *Lead with the courage of your convictions.*

E – *Engage others with your authentic self, leveraging your strengths.*

A - *Assess your mistakes and setbacks to move forward more effectively.*

D – *Drive diversity to ensure you have captured the best talent.*

E – *Extract learnings from every role along your career path.*

R – *Reflect on the feedback and input of others.*

I will explore each lesson in the framework in a dedicated chapter, highlighting the importance of each lesson with real-world examples. These examples will underscore the power of the lessons by both highlighting successes of leaders who embraced them and setbacks of leaders who ignored them. I trust these six leadership lessons will help you lead or contribute to your team and to your peers more effectively.

CHAPTER 1

L - *Lead with the courage of your convictions.*

E

A

D

E

R

"And it came to pass, when the Philistine arose, and came, and drew nigh to meet David, that David hastened, and ran toward the army to meet the Philistine."

"And David put his hand in his bag, and took thence a stone, and slang it, and smote the Philistine, and slew him …" (1 Samuel 17:48–49 [King James Version]).

My first recollection of David was not as a king of Israel, but as a brash young shepherd boy who courageously took on the giant warrior Goliath. He was a young man, passionately moved to action against an enemy. Scripture reveals that David was filled with righteous outrage toward Goliath, who had continuously mocked the nation of Israel. Many also inferred that David saw this as mocking God, which was entirely unacceptable. So, David convinced Saul, king of Israel, to allow him to represent the nation in battle.

I cannot fathom what those on the battlefield were thinking, as David took on this seasoned warrior. He was a combatant who struck fear in the hearts of even the most valiant of the fighting men. Did they think David was foolish, or simply reckless? How absurd is this situation—a young man, actually a boy, taking on the greatest of this fighting band of giants? And David moved forward without armor, a helmet, shield, or sword. He was armed only with what he knew worked for him: his staff, a bag filled with five stones, his sling, and a tremendous faith that

God would protect him. David was also armed with an incredible passion for what he was about to do. He was armed with the courage of his conviction that made him certain that he would prevail.

In my introduction, I indicated that my objective was to identify and extract several insights for leaders illustrated through experiences in David's life. The story of David and Goliath shines a spotlight on a leader's willingness to act and a willingness to take risks, both real and perceived, to advance the team's agenda and objectives. Because David had no formal organizational authority, it is clear that this dynamic applies to both leaders with and without formal authority. Like David taking on Goliath, both formal leaders and team members must have the courage to step out boldly into the fray, whether it be in a competitive, for-profit business environment or inside of a complex, not-for-profit environment. It takes not just confidence, but real strength of character to level a maniacal focus on a singular objective, especially when that focus may cut against the grain of normality and moves the organization out of its comfort zone. This focus must cause the leader to persevere in spite of resistance and organizational inertia pushing against them. David's singular focus on slaying the Philistine sets the stage for lesson number one:

Lesson #1: Lead with the courage of your convictions, demonstrating a maniacal focus on a clearly defined objective.

<u>Aligning People and Resources</u>

The CEO of 7-Eleven, for most of the past decade, has paid close attention to the consumer trends impacting retailers. Customers have been demanding more options: options for how they shop, how they receive their goods, and how they pay. He responded to these trends by moving 7-Eleven to develop digital platforms, with a customer loyalty application as the centerpiece of this effort. In late 2016, he decided to go all in. He would truly demonstrate the courage of his convictions by not just allocating resources in support of the work needed to become digitally enabled, but to *distort* resources to this effort. By distortion of resources, I mean he redirected resources from across the enterprise to this effort to rapidly accelerate 7-Eleven's digital capabilities.

What did this distortion of effort and resources look like? It began with establishing a digital team that would report directly to him. It included reshaping his "leader's intent," his statement of organizational purpose and direction, to signal to the organization how deep the commitment to building digital capabilities would be. The restated leader's intent was "to become a customer-obsessed, digitally-enabled enterprise, seamlessly linking brick and mortar locations with a suite of digital products, and services."

He convened his entire executive committee to examine how the culture of technology companies facilitate both customer obsession and speed to market. He overhauled the company's leadership principles to reflect principles more closely aligned with firms that relentlessly pursue customers' wants and needs. The company's leadership principles were augmented to add new elements such as:

- *Be Customer Obsessed: Start everything with the customer in mind.*

- *Be Courageous with Your Point of View: Robustly debate, align, and then commit.*

- *Challenge the Status Quo: Innovate, simplify, and constantly raise the bar.*

- *Act Like an Entrepreneur: Bust through bureaucracy; do more with less.*

Over the next four years, his relentless commitment to meeting the customer where they were heading resulted in initiatives that were on the leading edge for convenience retailing. Those initiatives included home delivery and mobile checkout. In less than four years, the initiatives moved beyond just leading edge for the convenience business toward leading edge across multiple industry sectors. Not only do nearly all US markets where 7-Eleven has a physical presence have home delivery across their entire metro areas, but 7-Eleven has the fastest delivery times across all home delivery platforms. That CEO had a big idea, and he pushed the organization with unwavering commitment toward bringing that idea to life.

The CEO had no idea that an international health crisis was on the horizon when he began this work. Nor, could he know how customer behaviors in a COVID-19 environment would change. But he did know where the customer was heading. The COVID-19 pandemic merely accelerated shoppers' desires for home-delivery options; touchless, contactless shopping environments; and a greater need for product purchasing discounts and values offered through the 7Rewards application. Consequently, the company, unlike many retailers, continued to thrive well into the pandemic. By passionately

17

pursuing this conviction of meeting the consumers at a place they were headed, his company continued to grow.

Facing Resistance

David, when he appeared at the battle site, was carrying bread and cheeses his father had directed him to deliver to the soldiers. When David arrived, impassioned by the love of God and inflamed by the courage of his convictions, he began trying to assert himself as the warrior Israel needed to face Goliath. But he was faced with ridicule and derision from many of the soldiers, including his own brothers. David's oldest brother, Eliab, angrily confronted him when he realized what David wanted to do. He said, **"Why camest thou down hither? And with whom hast thou left those few sheep in the wilderness? I know thy pride, and the naughtiness of thine heart; for thou art come down that thou mightest see the battle"** (1 Samuel 17:28 [King James Version]).

Resistance can come in many forms and be delivered from those who don't know you or your motivations well, or from those who you might think would understand you very well and be more supportive. Sometimes resistance will come because people do not understand the plan, trust in your ability to execute the plan, fear the status quo might change, or fear what that change may manifest for themselves. Imagine your own brother challenging your motives, and perhaps even your competence. Has anyone told you that perhaps you need to simply "stay in your lane"?

The resistance to a CEO can be a bit more subtle, but there was a good deal of it in this case. The whispers about this executive's big bet became louder grumbles as headcounts and budgets in many departments were scaled back in order to load up on his digital bet. Boldness couldn't take the shape of incremental movement, because the customers' expectations were changing at an unprecedented pace. Ultimately, his bold commitment to the approach, like David's bold commitment to his approach, yielded great success.

One might argue that this approach works for a chief executive who seemingly has the authority to marshal organizational resources and steer the team in any way they see fit. I would, in fact, concede that a CEO may have greater latitude to relentlessly pursue that big idea, but he or she is not exempt from organizational or cultural pushback. Don't forget, the CEO must also effectively navigate the heavy lifting required to align their board of directors.

Operating Against the Grain

When 7-Eleven's CEO established his new digital organization, the company already had one foot in the "self-checkout" camp. Self-checkout is found in most grocery stores and in larger format retail operations like Target and Walmart. Rather than check out at a register station staffed by a cashier who scans and bags your items, collects your money, and offers you change and a receipt, the shopper who chooses the self-checkout option does not engage a cashier. That shopper scans their own items, bags them, and inserts payment into an automated station. Retailers seemed to embrace this option as it allowed them to reduce the number of cashiers they would need to staff the operation, allowing them to either reduce their labor costs or redeploy that labor somewhere else in the business. 7-Eleven had self-checkout stations in pilot phase when the CEO established his digital team and the company was approaching the national rollout phase.

The CEO's charge to the digital team was to ensure the company was keeping pace with customer needs and expectations, not simply evolving technology in a linear fashion. Said more plainly, the customers didn't want a self-checkout option where they traded off standing in line for a cashier for standing in line to check themselves out. Even though the organization saw this as the logical next step in leveraging technology to satisfy the customer, customers had, in fact, leap-frogged the self-checkout station in favor of a mobile option. This option only required them to use their smartphones to check out.

Once again, the CEO confronted a powerful wave of resistance as he considered scrapping the developing self-checkout station initiative and pursuing the mobile, or frictionless option, which required the customer to stand in no line at all. Associates across the enterprise, including some senior-level personnel, questioned the prospect of this shift. Many challenged the quality of advice the CEO was receiving from his digital team, while questioning that team's business savvy and judgment both openly and in private discussions.

But the CEO had formed a powerful vision of where the customers were headed and how to meet them at that point. He was convinced that this was the appropriate path and he authorized the team to scrap a soon-to-be outdated approach for one that would resonate more powerfully with the customer. Today, 7-Eleven has deployed mobile checkout in hundreds of stores. As I previously noted, as COVID-19 fears escalated during 2020, 7-Eleven's customers were reassured by a touchless shopping option.

David felt righteous outrage at Goliath mocking both his God and his people. His strong conviction turned into a powerful motivation to act. 7-Eleven's chief executive was also driven by his strong desire to meet customers at the place they were heading. His conviction ignited a maniacal focus on satisfying the changing needs of customers. Like David, he acted on his conviction for the betterment of the organization he served.

I had a leadership professor at the University of Chicago once challenge me by asking, "Are you really making a difference or are you simply moving sand from one part of the beach to another?" Leading like David requires boldness of action when you are truly ready to make meaningful change.

Application Questions:

1) What are your convictions regarding your workplace?

2) How have these beliefs driven you to affirmatively make a difference?

3) What resistance are you encountering now or anticipating later?

4) How have you prepared to move forward despite the resistance you are encountering or anticipating?

CHAPTER 2

L – Lead with the courage of your convictions.

E – *Engage others with your authentic self,*

leveraging your strengths.

A

D

E

R

"And Saul armed David with his armour, and he put an helmet of brass upon his head; also he armed him with a coat of mail."

"And David girded his sword upon his armour, and he assayed to go; for he had not proved it. And David said unto Saul, `I cannot go with these; for I have not proved them.' And David put them off him."

"And he took his staff in his hand, and chose him five smooth stones out of the brook, and put them in a shepherd's bag which he had, even in a scrip; and his sling was in his hand: and he drew near to the Philistine" (1 Samuel 17:38–40 [King James Version]).

If you have been in the workplace a few years, you may have taken some sort of leadership assessment. There are many assessment tools in the marketplace, designed to help you gain insight into how you lead others, how you interact with others, and perhaps, what motivates or inspires you. While the Bible offers us no evidence that the young shepherd, David, had benefitted from any assessment instrument, he clearly knew much about himself. He also knew that he was skilled in the fighting tools of a shepherd, the staff and the sling. He understood his competitive strengths, and he also understood what his strengths were not.

David had protected his flock from both lions and bears using the tools and fighting techniques of a shepherd. He had not fought them using the armor and sword of a soldier. He understood that as he entered combat with the giant, Goliath, he would be well served using the tools and techniques he had mastered over the years. In this, the crucial moment, he relied on what he knew best rather than attempting to be someone or fight like someone he wasn't. David eschewed the personal combat gear of the king, because he was uncomfortable utilizing the traditional soldier's fighting approach. He knew his authentic self. The next leadership lesson is:

Lesson #2: Engage others with your authentic self, leveraging your natural or developed strengths.

Even before Shania Twain released a song with a similar title, I had already heard a saying in sports to "dance with the one that 'brung' you." This time-tested sports colloquialism signals that you are more likely to succeed leveraging tools,

27

techniques, and approaches you have spent time mastering. It also signals that it is risky to abandon them in favor of tools, techniques, and approaches you have not mastered in the crucial moment.

Let me continue with the sporting metaphor for a moment. Imagine a baseball player who typically hits for average and reliably gets on base at a high rate. Imagine that hitter, at a crucial point in a key game, trying to turn themselves into a home run hitter. It is certainly possible for the player to transform themselves into a different type of hitter, but that transformation will take a great deal of work and preparation. If that work had not already been done, they are more likely to be successful leveraging the skills that "brung" them to that moment. The authentic leader knows their strengths and leverages them for better results.

<u>Wearing Your Own Armor</u>

There was a regional manager for a large specialty retail chain that I worked with several years ago who took great pride in her coaching and development skills. When she visited stores across her region, she took satisfaction in connecting with all the stores' associates, from the newest cashiers and salespeople to the stores' management staff. She had a well-honed approach that included finding and reinforcing the good things that were going on in the stores, in addition to offering constructive feedback for improvement. She firmly believed that by reinforcing positive activity, the associates were more receptive to the constructive feedback she would also offer. Her region typically had both great morale and great results.

A reorganization of the stores' territories caused her region to be reassigned to a different zone vice president, one whose leadership style was very different. And while the new vice president was very knowledgeable of products and systems, it was clear to even the most casual observer that her approach to leading diverged from the regional manager's approach. The vice president was a lot more direct in challenging store personnel. She was not abusive or unprofessional, but she just chose to spend more time challenging the team to step up than reflecting on and reinforcing their successes. While her visits didn't always feel great, there was no doubt that she got people to respond and lift their games.

The new vice president compared her leadership style to the regional manager's style by sharing a metaphor using the very products sold in our stores. The vice president described the regional manager's style as "similar to a body lotion, which was smoothly applied to the skin. It could heal damaged skin, but the process did take some time." She then described her own style as "similar to a body loofah, which feels rough and granular when applied." The loofah, as she continued with the metaphor, "quickly removes the dead or unhealthy skin immediately, rather than simply soothing it in the moment while healing it over time." Her point was that while her approach in dealing with store associates was more abrasive, it drove results much faster than the more nurturing approach of the regional manager. And she believed the company needed to accelerate capturing greater results.

Unfortunately, the regional manager chose not to be her authentic self. Rather, she attempted to mimic her new supervisor's approach to capturing results. She became more abrasive when engaging her associates, and she spent less time delivering reinforcing praise in order to load up on constructive feedback. Of course, she had not spent years, or even months, refining this more challenging style when she adopted this change of approach. She simply saw that her new boss favored this style and she wanted to make her new boss happy.

While the change in her team's morale and the downturn in their results was not immediate, over the next year her region's performance began to steadily slide in the wrong direction. This was exacerbated by the increase in her region's employee attrition rate. Her attempt to deploy an approach she simply was not practiced at led her to exactly the opposite results she was looking for.

The point is not that one style is better than the other. The zone vice president had a very successful career. Her style worked for her. She delivered results. But the regional manager had not spent any time developing this approach. She simply abandoned the approach she had developed over time and had become quite proficient in for an approach that simply did not fit her. She abandoned her sling and stones to put on someone else's armor. She did not lead with her authentic self and her team paid a steep price.

Understanding Your Strengths

Let me offer an additional example that illustrates this principle at the organizational level. Some years before I had joined that specialty retail organization, I spent several years leading a small not-for-profit consultancy that engaged existing inner-city businesses to help them accelerate their growth. We did this by helping those business owners better understand and leverage their competitive advantages, pinpoint market growth opportunities, spot operating inefficiencies, identify growth and expansion capital, and other basic consultative services. We deployed either a direct engagement, where my staff or I would do the consulting directly with the business, or through an indirect engagement, where we would identify corporate professionals or university resources to consult with the small business.

Our sweet spot for success was engaging businesses that were three to five years old with annual revenues ranging from roughly $1 million to around $3 million. We were built to engage companies that had moved beyond start-up status and were seeking to better understand how they could accelerate their growth. My team's ultimate objective was to strengthen inner city-based businesses in order to create more jobs, income, and wealth for inner-city residents. I would tend to describe our effort as one part of an economic solution to inner-city distress, which of course, would complement other economic, social, educational, spiritual, and political efforts aimed at mitigating inner-city challenges. Our clients paid a nominal fee for our services, while large private foundations provided us the lion's share of our operating resources.

While we were fortunate enough to have some very large private foundations committed to funding our work, dollars were frequently tight and there was no room for inefficiency. As the managing director, I was constantly seeking additional partners to support our work. During my resource development work one year, I was connected to a large foundation that liked what we were doing and wanted us to expand our support services to include start-up and business incubator services for aspiring inner-city entrepreneurs. And in return, they offered us a healthy grant that could be renewed over several years. I accepted the grant and added this new direction to our already full agenda of work.

Remember, my team's core competencies revolved around skills needed to take a business that was already established and help them accelerate their growth. We were not well equipped to consult with start-up entities. The challenges confronting start-ups are typically very different from those of a more mature business, and I simply didn't have the resources or network established to venture into this new space. This just wasn't an organizational strength for us. It was not a part of our authentic selves as a team. We were attempting to wear the armor of an organization staffed and well-prepared to help aspiring entrepreneurs get started.

We did not succeed as a business incubator. Moreover, this additional focus area took away from our core mission by diverting essential resources from clients that were in our support sweet spot to clients that simply were not. And while the grant provided us some additional operating resources, it was not nearly enough to effectively reorganize the team or hire additional resources that could lead the new workstream. I tried to make us into something we simply were not and it made us less effective overall. So, after a tremendously difficult year, we did not pursue additional funding from that particular foundation. We stuck with what we knew best. We focused on being who we authentically were and, once again, were able to make a strong impact on our core clients and in the inner city that we served.

Over the years, I have embraced certain approaches that I have worked to hone to a high level of proficiency. I rely on those approaches to help me get traction with my leaders and teammates in order to consistently deliver high-level results. And as the previous example illustrated, even teams and organizations develop core capabilities and strengths. Leading authentically means understanding who you are, and how you can best add value. Leading authentically means you will not attempt to mimic the styles and approaches of others. Rather, you rely on those styles and approaches you have mastered, or at least those in which you have become most adept. Those are the styles and approaches that emerge like muscle memory and are part of your authentic self. The great jazz musician Miles Davis is credited with saying, "Sometimes it takes a long time to play like yourself." Miles clearly understood that developing your natural style takes time. I would add that when you have mastered that style, abandoning it can be perilous.

Now here is the disclaimer. I am *not* advocating being inflexible in your style or approach. Nor am I saying leaders should not develop new styles or approaches that allow them to grow and be more versatile. What I am saying is, leading with your strengths is better than leading with someone else's strengths. But once you have gained proficiency with new skills and approaches, you clearly become a more versatile leader. You become a leader with more tools in your tool kit. Once the team has gained new competencies, they become more versatile and valuable. They can then take on new and differing challenges.

David had developed a particular fighting style. He was not a guy who fought with swords and shields, while wearing a heavy suit of armor. At least at this stage of his life, that was not a part of his authentic self. Later, as he commanded great armies of Israel, he may have led and fought differently. But he knew who he was in the moment. He knew what his strengths were in the moment. And, he knew what worked best for him in the moment. He knew his authentic self and he showed up as his authentic self. Failing to embrace your authentic self can minimize your effectiveness.

Application Questions:

1) What are your most developed skills and strengths?

2) How are you leveraging those skills and strengths in your workplace?

3) What obstacles are preventing you from better utilizing your most developed skills and strengths?

4) How can you mitigate those obstacles?

CHAPTER 3

L – Lead with the courage of your convictions.

E – Engage others with your authentic self, leveraging
your strengths.

A – *Assess your mistakes and setback to move
forward more effectively.*

D

E

R

"And they set the ark of God upon a new cart, and
brought it out of the house of Abinadab that was in Gibeah:
and Uzzah and Ahio, the sons of Abinadab, drave the new
cart."

"And they brought it out of the house of Abinadab which was at Gibeah, accompanying the ark of God: and Ahio went before the ark."

"And David and all the house of Israel played before the Lord on all manner of instruments made of fir wood, even on harps, and on psalteries, and on timbrels, and on cornets, and on cymbals."

"And when they came to Nachon's threshing floor, Uzzah put forth his hand to the ark of God, and took hold of it; for the oxen shook it."

"And the anger of the Lord was kindled against Uzzah; and God smote him there for his error, and there he died by the ark of God" (2 Samuel 6:3–7 [King James Version]).

"And David was afraid of the Lord that day, and said, 'How shall the ark of the Lord come to me?'" (2 Samuel 6:9 [King James Version]).

There is an old saying that goes something like this: If you're digging yourself into a hole, *stop digging!* I have always valued this statement because it underscores two realities of life. The first reality is that we will all find ourselves making mistakes from time to time. I certainly hope that I don't make the same ones repeatedly, but I clearly know that I miss the mark on many things. If I start to forget that truth, my wife doesn't mind offering me a gentle, loving reminder of it.

The second reality is that we do not have to compound our mistakes once they have been made. We can "stop digging" in a number of ways, ranging from reevaluating our current situation to deploying new strategies or action steps going forward. David was not exempt from the human reality of being less than perfect. We know that while he was a great hero in the Bible, he was also a flawed and imperfect man. He was a man who made mistakes. In those cases where he stopped digging, reflected on his misstep, and adapted his plan to mitigate the earlier problems, he experienced even greater success. You and

I can also draw learnings from our failures and apply those insights to achieve greater success. While failing is unpleasant, you and I can use setbacks to improve our effectiveness. Our third leadership lesson underscores this dynamic:

Lesson #3: Assess your mistakes and setbacks critically to extract learnings to apply to your work going forward.

The context surrounding this lesson stems back to David's attempt to move the ark of God, a holy, ornately decorated, wooden chest that housed the stone tablets Moses brought down from Mount Sinai containing the Ten Commandments. When David, serving as king of a united Israel, had liberated Jerusalem from enemy hands he sought to move the ark to this important, capital city. However, God had provided very detailed instructions on not only how to move the ark, but who could move the ark. God's instructions for handling this sacred artifact were both detailed and inflexible. And David famously failed to execute his plan to move the ark correctly.

The results of this first attempt, as recounted in this chapter's introductory Scripture reference, were fatal. One of David's loyal men, Uzzah, died during this failed attempt. David disregarded the proper procedures for moving the ark, and he failed to ensure his men knew and understood the expectations. You could point to his failure to prepare his team properly, his failure to utilize the appropriate personnel (only Jews descending from the Tribe of Levi were authorized to transport the ark), and even his underestimating the gravity of the undertaking as all contributing to the failure. But once he had failed, he faced the challenge of learning from this failure in order to revive the undertaking more successfully.

Learning from Mistakes

Mistakes and failures can have severe, even tragic, consequences. But another tragedy that emerges from our setbacks and losses is a failure to learn from those setbacks, adjust our efforts appropriately, and move forward on a better course. Reflecting on our failures may cause us to determine a number of key factors that we may have misread, such as a lack of understanding of consumer needs, an underestimation of a competitive response or competitor's capability, or an underappreciation of the required preparation time needed to execute well. Sometimes we uncover a holistically flawed strategy. Failure can provide fertile ground for learning, and the best leaders I have been around understand this.

Years ago, I was a regional manager for a leading specialty retailer called Bath & Body Works. In that business, the holiday season that extends from November through New Year's Day led to disproportionately high sales in the stores. We often said sales for a day during the Christmas holiday season were like sales for a regular week, and sales for a week during the holiday season were like sales for a regular month. We took great pride in setting our stores with a holiday theme, while loading our in-store fixtures with plenty of gifting items. That particular year, the fronts of our stores were adorned with a huge plexiglass fixture shaped like a Christmas tree that was loaded with the hottest Christmas products. We called the fixture simply, the "plexi-tree."

On one particular day during the holiday season, I was visiting stores in Chicago with our senior vice president of stores and also the Bath & Body Works CEO. We walked into one store, greeted and chatted with the associates working, and took a look at what was selling and what was not selling. The items on the plexi-tree were moving rapidly, driving great sales for the business. As we moved to a wall fixture near the back corner of the store, the CEO grabbed an item off the shelf that had not been selling. He looked at it, then looked at both the SVP and me, saying, "I knew this wasn't going to sell when the merchants brought it to me." The SVP and I both turned to him with a puzzled glance that clearly spoke the words neither of us dared to actually utter: "Then why did you approve it?" The CEO, sensing our lack of understanding, answered our unspoken question aloud by simply saying, "How else were the merchants going to learn?"

That was a powerful moment for me—a moment when I clearly understood how much learning can emerge from every failure. On that day, the CEO of Bath & Body Works made it clear that he expects people to make mistakes, but he also expects them to extract lessons from those mistakes. He was such a believer in the power of learning from setbacks, that he allowed for a setback that he likely could have avoided because of the lessons that would emerge. It is, however, important to note that he also weighed the consequences of the failure to the business against the developmental opportunities for the merchants. There was a reason the item wasn't on the plexi-tree! He wanted the merchants to improve going forward, not to tank the critically important holiday sales season.

<u>Leaning into Learning Processes</u>

Learning organizations always leverage experiences, including ones that don't end well, to learn and grow. As a US Army officer, I vividly recall conducting "after-action reviews" after practically every activity. Oftentimes the learnings were much more robust when the mission was something less than an overwhelming success. Perhaps that is because the tendency of most leaders in organizations of all types is to engage in something less than a critically reflective assessment of an operation that yields great success.

Those after-action reviews were designed to build capability rather than to affix blame. At a minimum, we would review:

1) what was supposed to happen,

2) what actually happened,

3) why it happened,

4) how we do it better the next time, and

5) who should know about our findings and modifications.

Thoroughly exploring each step was foundational in effectively moving to the next step. For example, understanding why something happened (step 3) was designed to better inform our thinking to determine how to do it more effectively going forward (step 4). If, for example, the team determined during step 3 it made an error estimating the opposing forces' personnel strength, step 4 would include developing processes that ensure far more accurate assessments are made. The team was always better equipped to perform going forward after one of these deeply reflective learning processes.

Neither individuals, teams, nor organizations want to fail. But how you learn and apply the lessons of failure set the stage for future success. Do you remember the tragic E. coli contamination incidents involving a major fast-food burger chain back in 1993? Hundreds of consumers ingested contaminated meat in several Western states, and four young children even died from this contamination. Without belaboring the details of this tragic chapter in that company's history, investigators traced the outbreak back to undercooked burgers in the restaurants. This was a horrific failure.

However, that company did learn from its failure. In the aftermath of the 1993 tragedies, they placed a renewed emphasis on food safety. Some even argued that they reset the bar for food safety for the rest of the quick-service industry. They restructured their operating teams to more effectively teach, coach, and verify food safety. They are a better company today because they learned important lessons from their failure.

Similarly, the Bible tells us that David engaged in a great deal of prayer and reflection after his failure. David took a full three months developing his plan for his next attempt to move the ark. He learned from his previous failure and tended to every detail to ensure all involved in the operation were fully prepared to execute at a high level. His next attempt to move the ark of God was a tremendous success.

Failures happen. However, it is absolutely necessary for leaders to critically assess their setbacks in order to extract lessons for future, more effective performances. The reality is every one of us will fail in some way. I had a mentor once tell me that the guy who has never failed at anything has probably never accomplished anything of significance. Did you ever notice that most of the greatest home-run hitters in the history of major league baseball also fell victim to a lot of strikeouts? The point is simply this: don't be afraid of failure as they provide platforms for tremendous growth, development, and improvements.

Application Questions:

1) How has the fear of failure compromised your ability to effectively lead or serve your team?

2) What mechanism(s) do you have in place to extract lessons from your setbacks?

3) How have you helped your teammates to learn from their setbacks?

4) How are you sharing the lessons you learn with your teammates?

CHAPTER 4

L – Lead with the courage of your convictions.

E – Engage others with your authentic self, leveraging
your strengths.

A – Assess your mistakes and setback to move forward
more effectively.

**D – *Drive diversity to ensure you have captured the
best talent.***

E

R

"Again, Jesse made seven of his sons to pass before
Samuel. And Samuel said unto Jesse, The Lord hath not
chosen these."

"And Samuel said unto Jesse, 'Are here all thy children?' And he said, 'There remaineth yet the youngest, and behold, he keepeth the sheep.' And Samuel said unto Jesse, 'Send and fetch him: for we will not sit down till he come hither.'"

"And he sent, and brought him in. Now he was ruddy, and withal of a beautiful countenance, and goodly to look at. And the Lord said, 'Arise, anoint him: for this is he'" (1 Samuel 16:10–12 [King James Version]).

I introduced this chapter with Scripture that recounted how David was selected and anointed as the future king of Israel. The prophet Samuel had been instructed by God to find and anoint the future king. He was sent to visit the house of Jesse. But when Samuel arrived, Jesse trotted out his older sons, many of whom possessed a stature and countenance commonly associated at the time with royalty. But God commanded, **"Look not on his countenance, or on the height of his stature; because I have refused him: for the Lord seeth not as a man** seeth; for man looketh on the outward appearance, but the Lord looketh on the heart" (1 Samuel 16:7 [King James Version]).

Although you may have never used height or good looks as a criterion for selection, people and organizations do tend to limit their ability to field the very best team because of short-sighted hiring and advancement decisions. Our failure to be inclusive in our assessment and selection activity has created many formal leadership landscapes that are remarkably homogeneous. Formal leadership roles are still overwhelmingly filled by white males. When I completed my research on elements of workplace diversity for my doctoral dissertation nearly a decade ago, I found stark disparities between the numbers of racial minority leaders and white leaders throughout several business and government sectors. And even a quick scan of several more recent research efforts indicates scant progress has been made over the last decade. This dynamic exists despite overall workforces across America becoming less and less homogeneous overall.

It will become increasingly more difficult to win in business, or in not-for-profit environments, if you refuse to open your people decision-making aperture to a setting beyond simply those who act like, think like, or look like you. Moreover, limiting your people sourcing and selection practices to simply those sources and practices you are most familiar with will cause you to lose out on great talent. A more intentional focus on skill sets and leadership competencies coupled with a more deliberate effort at identifying new, untapped sources of talent will elevate the effectiveness of your team. Do you have a preconceived notion of the type of employee or teammate you want? Are you returning to the same well of talent again and again? The anointing of David, the most unlikely of individuals who could have been identified to lead, should challenge you to break the talent mold and to lead with the best people.

Lesson #4: Drive diversity to ensure you have captured the best talent.

Seeking Excellence and Finding Diversity

I recall a decade or so ago being hired to take over a division territory for a large, specialty retailer. I was hired during a major reorganization where the operating divisions were reconstructed, leading to an entirely new team of leaders being brought in. Part of the reorganization plan was for each new division leader to quickly assess their team of direct reports and make some tough decisions about who was going to remain on the newly redesigned operating team. Notwithstanding how difficult it is to make people assessments without any real observation time, I had to focus in on several elements of criterion. Of course, I poured through each person's historical performance, but I also recognized that those data points could possibly be skewed by several factors like the demographics of each territory, the talent level of the teams each individual inherited, and even the quality of sites in each individual market.

Rather, I wanted each person to articulate their vision, and recount for me how they communicated it, aligned their teams around it, developed supporting strategies and tactics, and iterated those tactics as their results emerged. Only then would I have a better line of sight to some of their critical skill set, to include their abilities to align disparate teams on performance goals, assess talent levels and develop individual performers, manage through the inevitable personnel conflicts, adjust to changing operating environments, and to steady the team through ambiguous situations.

My supervisor, along with my primary human resource partner, challenged me when one of my top selections was an Argentinian immigrant with a heavy accent and less corporate polish than many of his peers that I had on my interview slate. This guy, while not quite fitting into the mold that had historically been established for leadership at this level, clearly possessed the skill set that would lead to success quickly. Moreover, he appeared to have great upside for growth into higher-level roles, including the one I was in. Finally, he clearly possessed the spirit of a servant leader, along with an energy and drive that underscored his desire to set his team apart from the pack. When I bucked the trend and hired this leader, he not only excelled in his role, he was a perennial recipient of many of the company's top honors, including being named companywide Market Manager of the Year.

My team of direct reports and I formed the most racially diverse senior divisional operating team in the company. My team of reports was comprised of 33 percent African American leaders, 33 percent Latino leaders, and 33 percent white leaders. Nearly 30 percent of the team were women leaders. No other divisional team had less than 70 percent white or 80 percent male leaders. We stood out, not simply because we didn't look like the rest of the senior teams. We stood out because our performance results were consistently the best in the company. For two consecutive years my team was awarded the "Fire in the Belly" award, which recognized the top-performing division as measured by a scorecard of key performance metrics. The important thing to note here is that the team was comprised because of their skills and leadership competencies, not simply because they were racially diverse. But as a chief operating officer once told me: "If you seek excellence, you will find diversity!" In this case, his words could not have rung more true.

Expanding the Talent Net

While in the case I just described, I made very good talent calls, I also recognize that my own unconscious biases may have caused me to overlook talent and potential over the years. I remember traveling stores with one of my regional leaders one day, when we had stopped to observe customer interactions in a particular store. I immediately commented on how I probably wouldn't have hired one particular sales representative, as I found his tattoos and ear gauges off-putting. My field leader informed me that he was not only the top salesman in that store, but he was also among the top salesmen in the market. Customers loved him and frequently waited for him to become available to work through any problems or questions they might have been having with their product.

It was only after processing that information that I actually began to focus my attention on how effective that associate really was with customers. I remember thinking right then how I wished I had a crew filming a training video on how to effectively engage guests in our stores. But if I had been the hiring manager, I would have let my personal biases interfere with selecting top talent for our business. I had a perception about guys with tattoos and ear gauges that wasn't consistent with great guest service. Was I ever wrong! Thankfully, I had leaders in my organization who were not quite as myopic as I, who looked beyond the superficial to really understand the talents and gifts of potential associates.

Sometimes you will need to reshape your ideas around what talent looks like, sounds like and where you can find it. Once, while working for a worldwide "super-major" energy company in their supply chain function, I had the great pleasure of working alongside an African American colleague named Kimberly. Kimberly was a trained chemist from the University of Pittsburgh and she was whip-smart! Once, inside of a meeting we both attended that was populated mostly by white guys, someone asked about her background. When she replied that she was a chemist, the meeting leader remarked that he had never met a black chemist. Kimberly, barely containing her sarcasm, replied that he should stop by her office sometime because she had a whole directory of black chemists that he could review. Her point was clear. If you only look where you have always looked for talent, you could be missing out on some potentially great teammates.

Considering Different Styles

We can even be blinded by operating styles. We too often expect our teammates, particularly our direct reports, to think like and engage others in a way that mirrors our own thinking and styles. And the results of this intellectual blind spot can mean your team may not always be comprised of the best talent available. I will share a very personal anecdote that illustrates this notion.

As a multiunit field operating leader, I have been responsible for large groups of retail stores. During my very first experience as a multiunit field leader, I quickly realized that I could not physically be in more than one place at a time. So, no matter how great a retail operator I thought I was, if I was to propel my business forward, I was going to have to focus on building capacity in those I led. Simply put, I was going to have to help my teams develop skills and strengths that they could use to move the business forward whether I was there or not.

I work very hard to develop techniques and processes that build capacity. These processes begin with calibrating alongside my team members to ensure we are all aligned on what a good end state or result may look like. From there we may spend hours, and sometimes days or weeks, capturing insights on how performance gaps might have emerged. After we develop proficiency identifying and isolating underlying obstacles, I help my team build proficiency in developing remediation approaches that tie directly back to those underlying obstacles.

Because that "capacity-building" process can be time-consuming, many leaders in similar roles prefer a more expedient approach. I can recall interviewing with a hiring manager who was one of those leaders. During our discussion, he remarked how he led by pointing out the deficiencies and prescribing solutions. This style he described, which I characterize as the "tell-direct" approach, clearly has some benefits. It is a way for a leader to rapidly surface performance gaps and quickly get remediation activities in place. Those who engage in this approach will tell you that when they apply this method in a store, that store becomes more customer-ready more quickly. My question has been, and continues to be, what happens to those stores you are not in? Who is "fixing" those stores if you have never developed the deeper capacity in your teammates to identify gaps and execute remedies on their own?

Despite the reality that the teams I had led had overwhelmingly performed at the top of the charts in nearly every organizational key performance metric, that hiring manager told me that he was uncomfortable with my approach. He said he preferred leaders who could go into a store, point out the problems, and personally activate solutions. He went on to say that is what made him successful and what he wanted to see in those he hired or promoted. I remember walking away from that interview thinking I dodged a bullet. I suspected the teams formed there were limited by narrow paradigms of how leaders must think and act. I wondered if they would ever assemble the best possible team, or simply assemble a team that looked and thought like the hiring manager.

Suiting up the Best Players

The truth is that if your workforce is suboptimal, your output will be suboptimal. No matter what the context, you want to source and deploy the best talent available. Consider the coach of a local basketball team. If the team is populated with players who simply aren't very good, then it really won't matter if he paints the gym, buys new basketballs, or even outfits the team with brand new uniforms. Chances are, the team just won't win many games. Starting, however, with a quality base of talent can change the trajectory of the team's performance. And getting that quality base of talent may mean suiting up players from families who don't live on his street, or in his subdivision, or from his kids' school. That talent may not look like his kids. That talent may even come from a family who does not vote like he does, or worship like he does. But that talent will provide him with a stronger player base to coach.

Coaching and developing talent are inherent responsibilities of a leader. However, coaching and developing talent devoid of key skills or competencies causes that work to become a much slower, difficult process. I had a mentor challenge me once by asking, "How hard are you going to work to bring someone to average? What would happen if you invested that time you are spending with those who are less of a fit with associates who are a better fit for the role?" Her point was clear. Our team would move a lot faster and achieve better results if I start with the best folks I can find. And this dynamic may even be more critical in the not-for-profit sector, where organizational ineffectiveness or inefficiency can sound the organizational death knell very quickly.

Despite the intuitive truth surrounding the need for top talent, I still see leaders making decisions based on all sorts of things, except the right things. I have seen people make decisions based on sharing a common alma mater, a common fraternal connection, a common previous employer, a common ethnicity, or even common hometown roots. Sometimes one of those elements could actually play a role in helping you get to your final decision, but they should never supersede the foundational analysis of skills and competencies. Because I have a deep understanding of the leadership competencies the military attempts to develop in their leaders, I may have some greater insight into the experiences a military veteran applicant may have had exposure to. However, that applicant must demonstrate some level of mastery of those competencies before I simply sign off on him or her. Clinging to a single element, a superficial element, or an incomplete assessment will inevitably lead to less than desirable results. Even if the individual survives in the role, it is unlikely that the person will thrive.

Moreover, the "downstream" effect on people from underrepresented demographics is considerable. I have personally observed very talented women leaders leave organizations because they believed they had little chance of fulfilling career aspirations at organizations with few women in senior roles. I have seen this similar dynamic at work with underrepresented racial minorities as well. When this happens, the team not only suffers from potentially overlooking the best players for key roles, but their pipeline of future key players is compromised. This creates a double-whammy effect!

No one, at the time of David's selection, would have imagined he was the best choice to be the future king. After all, how could the youngest son of eight, relegated to shepherding duties, possibly have what it takes to lead a nation? Just as God was looking beyond the superficial and status quo, we need to look beyond as well. Choosing to look at every personnel opening as an opportunity to raise the talent bar will, sooner rather than later, elevate the entire team. And by expanding your sourcing net, to include more underrepresented people, you will be more likely to find the talent you seek. Remember, seek excellence and you will find diversity!

Application Questions:

1) How diverse is your leadership team? Does it reflect the diversity of your workforce or customer base? How can you change this?

2) Have you considered how new ideas, modes of thinking, and diversity of approaches can inject creativity and a new energy into your organization?

3) Where can you spread your net to source more diverse hires for your team?

CHAPTER 5

L – Lead with the courage of your convictions.

E – Engage others with your authentic self, leveraging your strengths.

A – Assess your mistakes and setback to move forward more effectively.

D – Drive diversity to ensure you have captured the best talent.

E – *Extract learnings from every role along your career path.*

R

"And Saul was afraid of David, because the Lord was with him, and was departed from Saul."

"Therefore, Saul removed him from him, and made him captain over a thousand; and he went out and came in before the people."

"And David behaved himself wisely in all his ways; and the Lord was with him" (1 Samuel 18:12–14 [King James Version]).

Imagine how difficult it can be to know you have been selected for a particular role, but must wait years, even fifteen years or more, to finally take on that role. David was thirty years old when he became king, yet theologians place him between ten and fifteen years old when he was anointed king by the prophet Samuel. That is a very long training and preparation period, during which he served in many roles. Even after learning of his future, David served as a shepherd, David fought Goliath, David served as the king's personal musician, David became a military leader, and eventually, David was installed as king. Yet, we know that in each stage of David's "career" he developed certain skills, gained greater wisdom, and even expanded his personal and professional networks, all of which would help him be more successful in his later role as king.

How often do we find ourselves stuck in a role we may not enjoy or believe underutilizes us? I think if we reflect honestly, we can all acknowledge having to pay some dues in a role that was a grind, or that we believed we were ready to move beyond. The more important question is what did you learn from those roles that you may have found yourself in along your career path? With every assignment you find yourself in, there are tools you can add to your tool kit that will make you more effective down the road. The fifth leadership lesson is:

Lesson #5: Extract learnings from every role along your career path.

While David was a shepherd, he developed an expertise with the sling while protecting his flock from lions and bears— expertise he would later apply in battle with Goliath. While serving as King Saul's personal musician, he learned a great deal about human nature, and became more adept at navigating political minefields. He also began to develop alliances, like with Saul's son, Jonathan, that would be critically important throughout his life. As one of Saul's military commanders, David developed both skill and confidence as a military leader. This experience would be critically important as he later commanded the armies of Israel against numerous military threats during his forty-year reign as king. He also began to identify the key leaders he would install as his advisors when he ascended to the throne. No experience was a wasted experience. No role was so insignificant that he took nothing away that would help him be more effective later. I think you could argue that he proactively looked to develop himself with every role of his career and in every stage of his life.

Losing Sight of Now While Looking for Next

At my current company, we have an extended field operational leaders' training and onboarding program. Depending on the particular trainee's level of retail leadership experience, this training can extend from just over a year to a full year and a half. The training is multifaceted, including classroom phases at our headquarters location in Dallas, and numerous field elements designed to ensure each new leader is grounded in store operations, the subtleties of merchandising effectively, developing effective product assortments, and planning and executing store and district level consultative activities. It is as comprehensive a training and onboarding program as I have ever been exposed to, with the possible exception of military training and onboarding.

This program can be either a good or not so good experience, depending on the participant's attitude toward it. Overwhelmingly, those who recognize the value of this extended preparatory structure soak in as much learning as possible while in the program, and perform at a very high level, nearly on par with experienced field leaders, from the moment they go live in the role they were hired for. However, we have seen a few field operational leader trainees grumble about the time they have to spend in a training status. They get so focused on finishing early that they fail to take full advantage of the opportunity they have to simply learn in a relatively stress-free environment. They lose sight of the reality that they can learn valuable lessons about the people, role structures, and challenges experienced by the very teams they may be leading when training is complete. They are, in fact, so busy looking forward they fail to optimize the opportunity of the space they are occupying at the moment.

But the dynamic I just described can be even more dangerous. The consequences of not pouring everything into a current role, of not learning and growing in place, can be more severe than just missing opportunities to get better; they can actually cause one to lose traction in one's current space. In short, performance might actually slide backward while one is looking forward. I remember working with a fairly seasoned regional leader while I was serving as a divisional vice president. As he was one of my direct reports, I was able to clearly identify his intellectual capacity, strong understanding of the business, great people skills, and clear upside ability. As is the case with all of us, he had a few developmental opportunities. But those opportunities were certainly minor in relation to his strengths. He clearly had strong potential for upward movement.

However, he was so anxious to get to the next level, he began to overlook critical pieces of his current role. I coached him on a few occasions to "be careful not to lose sight of *now* while you are focused on *next*." Yet, he continued to apply for seemingly every next-level role that opened up, whether it was something he was really interested in or not. He was constantly trying to set up informal interviews and "get-to-know-me" sessions. Don't misunderstand, each of you owns responsibility for managing your careers, and building a network is a key piece of that. But when those activities begin to supplant your focus on your current responsibilities, you have entered dangerous, even self-destructive, territory. Ultimately, this leader left the company frustrated that he wasn't being promoted faster. And the last I heard he had left several companies over the following thirty-six months still chasing that elusive promotion. I cannot help but imagine how successful he could have been at our company if he would have focused on learning and contributing as much as he could in that regional role, instead of being preoccupied with next.

Learning Wherever You Are Planted

When I entered the University of Chicago's MBA program a month shy of my thirty-fifth birthday, I had already commanded two separate artillery companies in the US Army, served as a director of operations and a member of the senior operating group for a national, full-service restaurant chain, and even launched and led a highly effective not-for-profit organization. I was a pretty seasoned leader by the time I graduated from business school at age thirty-six. Despite these experiences, I took my freshly earned MBA and entered Texaco's rotational leadership program for young business school graduates. Despite the reality that my practical experience was significantly more extensive than every one of my peers, I poured myself into the rotational program, eager to learn new skills and to capture new experiences that would serve me well later in my career.

I completed three rotational assignments over the next eighteen months, operating at lower levels than I was accustomed to but enhancing key skills I would apply later. As a business development manager in the Worldwide Power and Gasification business unit, I developed my ability to manage physical operating assets, determining the optimal power producing facilities to make additional capital investments in. As a business development consultant in one of ChevronTexaco's Technology Ventures' portfolio companies, I developed pricing models and the primary marketing plan for their hyperspectral sensing instrument (a device that would assist in identifying areas potentially rich with energy producing resources). As a financial analyst for yet another Technology Ventures' portfolio company, I created financial models that facilitated the CEO's assessment of potential joint ventures, as well as the impact of various incentive models and stock option plans.

Was I anxious to move to a "regular job" in the organization? I absolutely was. Was I anxious to resume working at a level more aligned with my more senior leadership experience? I absolutely was. But the financial acumen I developed and the analytical skills I honed have helped me more effectively lead at senior levels on my return to retail environments. Effectively deploying capital, determining ways to optimize my portfolio of store locations, and developing financial models integral to my zone's operating plans are just a few of the skills I was able to develop or strengthen during that eighteen-month rotation. I learned where I was planted, so that I could be more effective later.

I know there is a fine line between knowing when your career is stalling out and when the organization is allowing you to gain needed additional experience. I have personally made the decision to leave organizations where I thought my growth trajectory was limited. But even in those roles, with those firms I left, I tried to capture as many jewels of knowledge as I possibly could. I tried to augment my leadership and skills tool kit with new ideas and different approaches by observing and engaging my leaders, peers, and direct and indirect reports. And most importantly, I never once took my eye off my responsibility to deliver performance results in my existing role, whether I believed I was being underutilized or not. Like David, we all should seek learning and development at every stop on our journey to better prepare ourselves for better performances when we finally achieve our career objective, whatever that may be.

Application Questions:

1) While in your current role, what new skills can you develop to make you a more effective leader or contributor?

2) What existing skills can you deepen your mastery of in your current role?

3) Are you utilizing an individual development plan to map out developmental opportunities for yourself? What feedback have you gotten from your supervisor, peers, or direct reports on development opportunities? How have you incorporated that feedback into your individual development plan?

CHAPTER 6

L – Lead with the courage of your convictions.

E – Engage others with your authentic self, leveraging your strengths.

A – Assess your mistakes and setback to move forward more effectively.

D – Drive diversity to ensure you have captured the best talent.

E – Extract learnings from every role along your career path.

R – *Reflect on the feedback and input of others.*

"And Joab fought against Rabbah of the children of Ammon, and took the royal city."

"And Joab sent messengers to David, and said, I have fought against Rabbah, and have taken the city of waters."

"Now therefore gather the rest of the people together, and encamp against the city, and take it: lest I take the city, and it be called after my name."

"And David gathered all the people together, and went to Rabbah, and fought against it, and took it" (2 Samuel 12:26–29 [King James Version]).

Let me start by offering a bit of context for the Scripture that opens this chapter. Joab, David's primary military commander, had been leading the army of Israel against national threats on the battlefield, while David was neglecting his duties as the warrior king, living comfortably back in his palace in Jerusalem. And while Joab was capturing military successes, he also recognized that David's place was with his army while they were at war. I cannot say with any certainty what Joab's motivation was. Was he really planning on naming a captured city after himself rather than his king? Or, did he fear for the morale of the soldiers who noted the conspicuous absence of their king? Whatever his motivation, he clearly intended to send a wake-up call to his absentee monarch. And while David could have responded badly by taking punitive action against Joab, he responded by heeding Joab's advice to get back to work. Hopefully, this final insight from David's life and experiences has become clear:

Lesson #6: Reflect on the feedback and input of others, including subordinates, peers, and partners.

Listening to Alternatives

For many of us, whether we are in formal leadership roles or not, listening to the perspectives of others can be difficult when they diverge from our own perspectives. Perhaps we struggle with this because we all tend to view ourselves as having good ideas that can and should carry the day. Listening well can be even more challenging when there is feedback coming your way that may move beyond just a critique of your ideas, but a critique of your performance approach, your attitude, or your level of engagement. But working to truly hear the input and feedback of others, and then to engage in meaningful reflection on that input, can help you to uncover personal blind spots and move forward with a better-informed point of view.

But what do I mean when I say it is important to reflect on feedback? Am I referencing some extended process that can diminish your impact by delaying execution? Not at all. The process of reflection that I point to is one where you consider both the upside and downside of proposed alternatives, while applying your understanding of the situation, which may include factors like the competitive set, the operating environment, your own strengths, and your own opportunities. The combining of your personal assessment of the situation with the feedback offered to you from knowledgeable others can help lead you to decisions that improve your likelihood of achieving the desired result. Yes, this *can* be an extended formal process, where you employ decision matrices and other tools, but it *can also* be a quick calculation in your head, where you quickly do the reflection and analysis on the fly.

Consider if you would a football coach whose team has just scored but is still trailing by a point with under two minutes left in the game. Should the coach call for an onside kick, hoping to recapture possession and drive for a game-winning score? Or, should he call for a normal kick-off, and rely on his defense to pin his opponents quickly, giving his offense another chance to score. There is no time for a formal team meeting. But the coach will quickly process the upside and downside of his options. If an onside kick is successful, his team is better positioned to win. If it fails, the opponent's chances of winning improve. His key assistants will offer their perspectives even while the coach considers factors like how well his offense and defense has been playing, how well his opponent's offense and defensive has been playing, and even how many time-outs he owns to stop the clock. And all of this will be processed in seconds.

If you are not a football fan, perhaps you found the previous metaphor confounding. Suffice to say processing feedback can even be done in the moment feedback is offered. You do not have to engage in extended or cumbersome processes to use feedback effectively. Feedback can and should be processed real-time if the situation demands it.

You will note that I didn't say it is important to generate some action (beyond reflection) for every piece of feedback you get. Your reflection process may still result in you dismissing another's perspective. In an earlier chapter I discussed the 7-Eleven CEO listening to and reflecting on input regarding the dangers of his approach. However, he made the courageous decision to move decisively in accordance with his convictions. In that scenario he plowed forward successfully, but only after listening to other points of view and evaluating the merits of those points of view. Listening to alternate perspectives improves your decision-making by helping you better understand the breadth of potential outcomes. Only then can you make the highest-quality decisions.

Establishing a Safe Environment

It is also important that the environment we create or operate in is one where others feel safe in offering their perspectives. Leaders who have created an environment where others do not feel comfortable sharing feedback or an opposing point of view are setting themselves up for failure. Blind spots are called that because we cannot see them ourselves and we don't know they are there. Trusted colleagues who we allow to provide us unfiltered feedback, coaching, advice, or to simply keep us accountable are critically important.

But creating an environment where others feel safe in delivering feedback is not always as simple as it may appear.

Even those of us who think we understand how important feedback is might have inadvertently created barriers that keep others from honestly sharing their perspectives with us. Let me share an example where, if not for a very courageous colleague, I might have moved forward believing I was receiving, real, unfiltered feedback from my team when I actually wasn't.

At the end of every accounting year, our enterprise stages a huge conference in Las Vegas for our thousands of franchisees and corporate store operating teams. It provides a tremendous opportunity to review organizational strategies, preview major initiatives, learn about new selling platforms and products, and celebrate the accomplishments of the enterprise. Traditionally, every operating zone has its own rewards dinner in which they honor those individuals who really distinguished themselves through their performance throughout the year. As a zone leader, I looked forward to celebrating with my zone colleagues and honoring special individuals who made the most impactful differences in our business.

In preparation for the zone dinner one year, I convened my team of direct reports and support staff partners to discuss who had really distinguished themselves beyond just our balanced scorecard. My plan was for us to discuss and agree on which leaders I would recognize at our zone dinner with one of several special achievement awards, the newcomer of the year, and the very prestigious field consultant of the year honor. That year, absent from my slate of awards was a market manager of the year recognition.

Our market managers are regional leaders who report directly to zone leaders. These important business leaders, who lead business units that generate more than $200 million in merchandise sales every year, lead teams that can include ten or more direct reports and one hundred or more stores. They manage multiple product categories, a fuels business that generates millions of additional dollars in revenues, and effectively engage both external supplier partners and numerous internal support functions. These leaders, who have to be both tactically proficient in store-level operations and strategically sound in leading these large business units, are essential to successfully achieving our objectives.

I explained my rationale for not wanting to single out a sole market manager for recognition. As senior leaders inside of the zone, I wanted to ensure they operated collaboratively. I didn't want to create any incentives that might cause them even a moment of hesitation in sharing best practices or lifting up a peer across the zone. And since there was a monetary award connected with each honor, I suggested we could repurpose that award and its associated dollars for an additional award for a frontline associate. In hindsight, I believe my thinking was flawed but I articulated my position that day clearly and confidently. I then asked the team, which included not only the seven market managers but an additional seven key members of our zone's support staff, for feedback. As I scanned the conference room for a dissenter, I saw only heads nodding in agreement. Even my human resource leader, who I relied on to keep me from doing anything short-sighted regarding our people, seemed aligned.

Just as I was about to move to another agenda item, one of the newest members of our senior staff stopped me to offer her concerns with my short-sighted plan. Barbara told me that recognizing the top-performing market manager was not simply an honor for that leader, but it was a powerfully motivating recognition for everyone working on that market team. Every field consultant, franchisee, store manager, and sales associate in that market would celebrate the recognition of their market manager as an acknowledgment of the entire team's efforts. Her position reminded me of how the whole division celebrated together when I accepted the "Fire in the Belly" award back in my specialty retail days.

As Barbara thoughtfully and courageously articulated her opposition to my plan, I noticed one or two heads that seemed to nod in agreement. Recognizing the chilling effect the up-front articulation of my perspective had on the team's willingness to offer unfiltered feedback, I knew I would need to reset. I reminded the team that the guy with the highest position grade in the room does not always have the right answers, and that I was relying on each of them to help me make the best decision for the team. Consequently, I went around the room again, this time asking each individual directly for their opinion on my plan to exclude a market manager of the year award. Unanimously, the team believed recognizing a top market manager would be the right thing to do. And they were absolutely right.

Getting the awards dinner recognition piece correct was important, but even more important to me was recognizing that I had a lot more work to do to ensure every member of the team felt empowered to offer me feedback, to courageously provide their points of view when we were developing various courses of action. Clearly, I had more work to do in building levels of trust between each of them and myself. I also recognized that I would have to do a much better job in soliciting feedback from every member of the team, and in discussing their points of view whenever they might be offered. Creating a safe environment for others to offer feedback is a critical element of listening well.

Valuing All Perspectives Regardless of Grade Status

But listening well needs to extend far deeper than just that layer of direct reports or staff leaders you interact with regularly. Listening well requires you to engage team members at various levels of the organization, as their perspectives will also inform better decision-making. Their vantage points oftentimes allow for greater insights than yours might readily allow.

Let me share another personal experience that underscores the importance of listening to inputs from all members of the team, no matter their grade level or tenure. Years ago, I worked as a director of operations for a large full-service restaurant chain. My role placed me on a team known as the senior operating group. This team, which met biweekly at our headquarters location in Nashville, included the senior vice president of stores, three area vice presidents, and two directors of operations, of which I was one. We discussed issues facing the brand and ways to accelerate the business, which had been in decline for several years. The team had devised a scheme to improve kitchen efficiency, which included repositioning several pieces of equipment along the cookline.

To execute this plan, we charged the facilities team to reposition gas and electrical lines, and to reposition both large refrigeration equipment and large cooking equipment across the system. As you might imagine, the disruption in our kitchens that was needed to execute these changes was significant, as was the actual dollar cost of the work. To say this was a huge effort would be a bit of an understatement. This was an enormous undertaking of time and expense.

The only problem was, for every cookline efficiency that was created by the changes, there was at least one inefficiency that emerged. In fact, the new inefficiencies overshadowed the positive changes that the effort was designed to capture. Ultimately, the organization was so displeased with the outcome of the redesign that it actually spent an equal amount of time, energy, and money to reverse the process, restoring stores to the original cookline configuration. Clearly, one glaring failure was choosing not to test the proposed change with a small number of stores before launching an enterprise initiative. Just as egregious a miss, however, was our failure to listen to our cooks' perspectives on the proposed changes to their workspace before the initiative commenced.

I remember talking to a line cook in the back of one of our Kansas City area stores after both the work and the rework had been completed. He asked me with complete sincerity, "Why didn't you guys talk to me before you made those changes? I could have told you what was going to happen. I think most experienced cooks could've told you the very same thing."

That discussion with the cook provided a powerful insight that changed my perspective on how I would conduct business going forward. I have literally made over a thousand store visits since that moment in Kansas City. On every single one of those visits I talk to frontline associates about their thoughts on our business initiatives, the obstacles impacting their ability to meet and exceed performance objectives, and ideas they have that will help us better serve our customers and store teams. I learned a tremendous lesson in that Kansas City kitchen. We can learn, grow, and improve by listening to everyone on the team, including peers, supervisors, direct and indirect reports, and especially those teammates operating closest to our customers.

My current organization works hard to listen to all of its stakeholders before plowing forward with any initiative. We have forums where franchisees' perspectives are aired, and other frameworks where field operators across multiple levels are pulsed for their perspectives on both existing and potential organizational initiatives. In fact, while working as a support function leader at our headquarters, I frequently heard our CEO ask me and other support function leaders who presented him an idea, "What did operations say about it?" His message, in that simple question, is clear. Ensure you are listening to those who are most impacted by your ideas.

Listening to those around you is critical for success. It enables you to develop a more complete understanding of your situation. Regardless of your role on the organizational chart, nobody has complete line of sight into how various decisions, policies and practices, or initiatives will impact every stakeholder. Even those situated at the most senior levels of teams will have to work to ensure they are capturing feedback from those players closer to the front lines to truly understand how that great new idea is really affecting the team's ability to achieve its objectives. Seeking feedback from others is important at every level. But equally important is ensuring you are operating in an environment where others feel safe bringing you feedback, even when that feedback is unsolicited. There is truth in that adage about feedback being a gift. And as we have seen in the experiences of David, leaders must be prepared to receive that gift.

Application Questions:

1) What mechanisms have you identified and created to ensure you are capturing the feedback of direct reports or peers before you launch an idea or initiative?

2) What process have you established to ensure you can capture personal feedback on your performance or impact? How have you leveraged the concept of an accountability partner?

3) How safe do your direct reports or peers feel in providing you unfiltered feedback? What can you do to create an environment where they may feel more comfortable doing so?

SUMMARY

I have always found the life and experiences of David compelling. Even with his very human flaws, I look to his life as one that personified faith and obedience. But as a student of leadership, and a veteran manager who has served in many types of organizations, I am completely fascinated by the leadership lessons that his life experiences highlight.

Let's do a quick review of the six lessons in this book:

Lesson #1: Lead with the courage of your convictions, demonstrating a maniacal focus on a clearly defined objective.

Leaders, whether formally assigned or informal influence brokers, must courageously move the team toward those initiatives that they see as most impactful. Expect resistance, especially if you have a view that is counterintuitive, or a perspective that is just simply outside of the box of traditional thinking. Your efforts could very well mean the difference between incremental growth of the team and transformational growth of the team. This takes courage. This takes commitment. But making a substantive difference is always worth the effort.

Lesson #2: Engage others with your authentic self, leveraging your natural or developed strengths.

You have spent years developing a set of skills or honing an approach for effectively engaging others. Leverage those efforts by deploying those highly developed skills or proven approaches to engagement, rather than mimicking approaches that are less than authentic for you. Leading with your authentic and genuine strengths can propel you and your teammates through the many difficult challenges you face. There is a caveat. Please do not mistake leading authentically with being inflexible or not being open to augmenting your skill set or style of approach. There is always value in building out your tool kit. Even my favorite football team, Army West Point, mixes in a pass or two while leveraging their strength as a running team. But lead with what you do best. Your authentic self is typically your best self.

Lesson #3: Assess your mistakes and setbacks critically to extract learnings to apply to your work going forward.

We should learn from both successes and failures. Holistic reflection on those setbacks can set your team up for accelerated success moving forward. Wallowing in setbacks is not healthy. But investing the necessary energy to better understand what you may have overlooked, miscalculated, or even failed to execute crisply will inform your subsequent efforts. Don't be afraid of failures. Embrace them as the learning opportunities that they really are.

Lesson #4: Drive diversity to ensure you have captured the best talent.

No matter how you slice it, you cannot be successful without great talent. A great coach will struggle with subpar players. A great plan will yield no better results than a poor plan if you don't have talent that can execute well. The real question is, are you really seeking out the best talent? Or are you simply populating your workforce, or even your immediate team, with talent that looks like, acts like, and thinks like the status quo? Looking beyond the superficial, for real depth of skill set and alignment with needed competencies is not as easy or intuitive as one might think. Our staffing habits, like every other habit in the workplace, is subject to our old thinking, and our unconscious biases. Diversity of thought and background is healthy. And it lifts the quality of our decision-making and our execution. Be very deliberate in spending the additional time needed to really spread your net to find the best players.

Lesson #5: Extract learnings from every role along your career path.

Whatever you want your final destination in your organization to be, you will likely have to spend time in lower-level or developmental roles. Make the most of that time. There are skills you can hone, approaches you can develop, networks you can establish, and a host of other benefits you can capture while you are in those roles. Consider the time you spend in those roles as learning opportunities, which will ultimately make you a more effective leader. Don't get caught looking ahead, as you will miss those learning opportunities and even sabotage yourself if you fail to deliver in a developmental role you occupy while moving along your career journey.

Lesson #6: Reflect on the feedback and input of others, including subordinates, peers, and partners.

No matter how smart or experienced you are, there are people working around you with valuable insights that can and should inform your thinking. Getting caught in that trap where you find yourself only listening to those working at or above your grade level leaves you susceptible to lower quality decision-making. Everyone in your organization has a point of view about areas they are immersed in and disregarding those points of view can be costly in both time and money. Listening is about capturing a more complete view of the situation. Listening helps you become more aware of your biases and blind spots. And while your original ideas may still carry the day, when you have a more holistic understanding of the context, you can be more confidant in the decisions you ultimately have to make.

A Final Thought

The six lessons we have discussed are actually not new ideas. Rather, they are leadership truths that have existed in some form or another since the dawn of organizations. But seeing how important they were, even centuries ago in the life of David, underscores how important they remain today. I hope my personal anecdotes offered in each chapter have illustrated how crucial these lessons have been for me. I have been able to lead and contribute more effectively when I put the lessons into use. Conversely, I have experienced workplace setbacks when I have overlooked them.

I hope that presenting the six lessons inside of the LEADER framework resonates with you. Moreover, I hope this book causes you to reassess how effectively you have embraced the lessons in your role as a formal leader or as an individual contributor on your work team. Ultimately, I want you to reflect on how you can meaningfully incorporate these lessons into your workplace. David was a flawed man who God used to accomplish great things. We are also imperfect leaders, but we can be more effective in our roles by leaning into these lessons captured from the experiences of David and articulated in the LEADER framework.

ABOUT THE AUTHOR

Larry Hughes has spent the last 12 years serving in various leadership roles with one of the world's largest retailers, 7-Eleven, Inc. While at 7-Eleven, he has led division and zone level business units in both the Pacific Northwest and Southwest regions of the United States. As a Vice President of Operations, he has been responsible for managing the profitable sales of business units generating more than $2 billion annually. He has also served 7-Eleven as Vice President of Franchise Systems, responsible for development of franchise policies, franchise sales, and franchise owner engagement platforms. Additionally, Hughes has served as Vice President of Learning and Development, responsible for the design and delivery of all training initiatives at 7-Eleven, as well as organizational leadership and diversity initiatives.

Hughes, a veteran of the United States Army, continues to serve military families as a board member of the Armed Services YMCA. He is also serving the State of Texas as a member of the Physician Assistant Board. He and his wife of more than thirty years, Angela, are active volunteers with Bible Study Fellowship in the North Dallas area. They also continue to shepherd their sons, Geoffrey and Garrett, who are both completing their undergraduate degrees.

Larry earned his Doctor of Education in Human and Organizational Learning from the George Washington University. He earned his Master of Business Administration in both Strategy and Managerial & Organizational Behavior from the University of Chicago. He also holds a Master of Science in Management from Baker University in Kansas. He is a graduate of the United States Military Academy at West Point and a proud member of Kappa Alpha Psi Fraternity, Inc.

Made in United States
Orlando, FL
09 July 2023